W9-BTK-663

WILDLIFE RESCUE

Black Bear Rescue

By Glen Phelan
Illustrated by Tom Newsom

PICTURE CREDITS
3 (top left), 3 (bottom right), 5 (bottom left),
5 (right), 44 (top left), 45 (right), 46 (top
left), 46 (bottom), 48 (top left), 48 (bottom)
© Photodisc Green/Getty Images; 3 (top
right), 4 (top right), 44 (top right), 47 (top),
48 (top right) © Corbis; 44 (bottom) Mapping
Specialists, Ltd.; 45 (top) © Tim Fitzharris/
Minden Pictures; 46 © Philippe Clement/
Nature Picture Library; 48 (center)
© D. Robert & Lorri Franz/Corbis.

**PUBLISHED BY THE NATIONAL
GEOGRAPHIC SOCIETY**
Produced through the worldwide resources
of the National Geographic Society, John M.
Fahey, Jr., President and Chief Executive
Officer; Gilbert M. Grosvenor, Chairman of
the Board.

**PREPARED BY NATIONAL GEOGRAPHIC
SCHOOL PUBLISHING**
Sheron Long, Chief Executive Officer; Samuel
Gesumaria, President; Francis Downey,
Vice President and Publisher; Richard Easby,
Editorial Manager; Anne M. Stone, Editor;
Margaret Sidlosky, Director of Design and
Illustrations; Jim Hiscott, Design Manager;
Cynthia Olson, Ruth Ann Thompson, Art
Directors; Matt Wascavage, Director
of Publishing Services; Lisa Pergolizzi,
Production Manager.

MANUFACTURING AND QUALITY CONTROL
Christopher A. Liedel, Chief Financial Officer;
Phillip L. Schlosser, Vice President; Clifton M.
Brown III, Director.

CONSULTANT
Mary Anne Wengel

BOOK DESIGN
Steve Curtis Design, Inc.

Published by the National Geographic Society
1145 17th Street N.W.
Washington, D.C. 20036-4688

Product #4U1005099
ISBN: 978-1-4263-5092-4

Printed in Mexico.

11 10 09 08 07
10 9 8 7 6 5 4 3 2 1

Contents

The Characters

Wildlife Rescue is a company that helps wild animals. They take care of animals who are sick, injured, or in danger. When the animals are ready, Wildlife Rescue returns them to the wild. This is never an easy task. Each rescue becomes an adventure. It takes our group of heroes all over the country. From the forests of the Northeast to the shores of the West Coast, Wildlife Rescue is ready to roll.

Victor Montoya is an animal expert at the County Zoo. He is also part of the Wildlife Rescue team that travels the country helping wildlife in trouble.

Susan Montoya is a veterinarian (an animal doctor). She treats injured and sick animals at the County Zoo. As a member of the Wildlife Rescue team, Dr. Montoya treats animals in the wild.

Angela Montoya is 11 years old. She hopes to be a vet like her mom. Angie likes to travel with her parents when they go on wildlife rescue missions.

Jonathan Montoya is Angie's nine year-old brother. He asks a million questions because he always wants to learn more about animals.

Jason Tenbrook works for the United States Forest Service. He is a wildlife biologist and studies how animals behave. Jason also takes care of wounded animals until they can be released back into the wild.

CHAPTER 1

Backyard Visitors

Lauren Martin stared out the open kitchen window. She thought she had heard something. It sounded like a sniffle, or a grunt. Maybe it was just the breeze.

Night had fallen, but the kitchen light cast a glow out into the yard. She could see their swing set on the grass. She could see the maple tree in the corner of the yard and the bird feeder hanging from a low branch. She could even see a little bit of the woods at the back of the yard. But she couldn't see the pair of eyes peeking out of those woods. . . .

Lauren started to turn away from the window. Then she saw something move. She looked back in time to see a shape dash across the yard toward the tree. Whatever it was, it was big and black. Then she saw it clearly. It rose up on two thick, furry legs. WOOSH! With a mighty swing of its paw, the plastic bird feeder came crashing down. Sunflower seeds burst out all over the grass.

"Mom, Dad, there's a bear in the yard!" Lauren yelled.

Her parents hurried into the kitchen. "Where?" asked her dad.

Lauren pointed toward the tree. Then she turned and yelled upstairs. "Hey Claire! Max! Come look at the bear!"

"Quiet," said Mrs. Martin. "You'll scare it."

Claire and Max came running. "Where's the bear, where's the bear?" asked a delighted Max.

Lauren helped her four-year-old brother onto the kitchen counter so he could see out the window. Max's eyes widened.

The bear had eaten most of the seeds. Now it was poking its nose into the broken bird feeder. Its huge paws held the feeder as its tongue lapped up the seeds. The children giggled.

The bear sniffed around the ground for other seeds. Suddenly it lifted its head and looked right at the Martins. Lauren smiled at its big, brown eyes. Then it turned and ran back into the woods.

"Yea! A real live bear!" Max jumped down from the counter and clapped his hands with glee.

Mrs. Martin was not as thrilled. "I think we should call the police," she said to her husband.

He shrugged. "I suppose. But what good will that do. The bear's gone."

Just then, something else caught their attention. They had been watching the news, and the TV was still on in the family room. Suddenly they heard their town mentioned. They went into the family room. The TV news reporter was talking.

". . . That's right—black bears. These animals have been sighted near some towns south of Albany. The towns' police chief says he expects more sightings in the future."

The scene switched to an interview with their town's police chief.

"We're very close to the Catskill Mountains here in upstate New York," the chief said. "And the Catskills are bear country. If people see a bear in town, they should call the police immediately."

The news reporter continued. "Experts say that the bears are especially active this time of year. They've been sleeping all winter long, and they are hungry. So keep the lids on your garbage cans. Now in other news. . . ."

Mrs. Martin went straight to the phone and called the police. She wasn't the only one. The police received more than 20 calls about bears that night. There was no great damage, and no

one got hurt. However, people found out that a tightly sealed garbage can is no match for a hungry black bear. The bears had ripped the lids off several cans.

The bear sightings continued the next night . . . and the next. It was clear that the problem wasn't going to go away. So the mayor called a special meeting to discuss the issue. Many townspeople showed up, including the Martins.

The meeting opened with an update from the mayor. She displayed a map of the town.

Black dots showed all of the bear sightings. Most of the dots were on the south side of town.

"There are about 50 dots here. Of course, we don't have 50 bears. Many sightings are of the same bear. I'd say we're talking about 5 to 10 bears. We've been scaring them away, but they keep coming back."

"Why don't ya just shoot 'em?" came a voice from the back of the room.

A lot of people nodded in agreement. "That's certainly one solution we'll have to consider," said the mayor.

Lauren and Claire couldn't believe it. They wouldn't really kill the bears, would they?

But the townspeople were concerned. Was it safe for their children to play outside? Were pets safe? What kind of damage could the bears do? Could they be caught?

Lots of questions . . . but no answers.

Then someone said, "We all know something has to be done. The question is 'What'? I agree with the man who spoke earlier. It's legal to hunt bears. Why don't we have a bear hunt?"

Claire shuddered. She remembered one time when hunters passed them on the road. She saw a dead bear in the back of their truck. It made her feel sick.

"I think we're going too fast," said the mayor. "There may be only a few bears. There must be something we can do besides kill them. I think we need to get some expert advice."

That got Lauren thinking. Suddenly her eyes widened. She whispered something quickly to Claire. Lauren was so excited that she yelled out. "We got it! We got it! Wildlife Rescue!"

CHAPTER 2

A Job for Wildlife Rescue

Everyone turned to look at Lauren. "What's Wildlife Rescue?" the mayor asked.

Lauren stood up and shyly explained. "They are wildlife experts. I think they work at a zoo, in Missouri. They travel all over the country to help animals. They take care of them if they're sick or hurt. Sometimes they move wild animals to places where they don't bother people. I know they've worked with bears before."

"How do you know so much about them?" Lauren was excited now and spoke fast. "My sister and I are taking a class at the nature center. We're learning how to help injured animals. Mostly birds. Anyway, a couple of weeks ago, Mr. Montoya from Wildlife Rescue came and talked to the class. He's terrific. I know he'd come back to help us. I just know it."

It was worth a try. The mayor and the town council voted to contact Wildlife Rescue.

Victor Montoya had his hands full. Full of porcupine, that is. He was showing this prickly animal to a group of children at the zoo. They wanted to pet it, but that wasn't a good idea.

"This little fella looks cuddly, doesn't he? But he's covered with 30,000 sharp quills. Each quill is like a little spear. That's how he protects himself. If another animal tries to attack, it gets stuck with the quills."

The children had lots of questions. Mr. Montoya answered them all. Soon it was time to put the porcupine back in his cage.

As he was closing the cage door, his cell phone rang. "Who could this be?" he wondered.

"Hello. Victor Montoya here."

"Hello, Mr. Montoya. My name is Cindy

Garland. I'm the mayor of a small town in upstate New York, and am I glad to talk to you. . . .

The mayor filled him in. They talked as he walked across the zoo grounds.

Just as he said goodbye to the mayor, a familiar voice came from behind.

"Hey, Dad!"

Mr. Montoya turned to see his son, Jonathan, running toward him. His daughter, Angela, followed close behind. "Dad, guess what?" Jonathan said.

"What?"

"We put the bunny back in the nest, and the mother is taking care of her!"

Angela and Jonathan had been taking care of a young injured rabbit. She had cut her leg badly on the bottom of a chain link fence. With the help of their parents, they nursed the rabbit back to health. They cleaned the wound. They kept her safe and fed until the wound healed. Today, they put her back where she belonged.

"I have news too," Mr. Montoya said.

Angela's eyes opened wide. "Really? What?"

"I'll tell you in a minute. Let's go find mom."

"Oh come on Dad," Jonathan complained.

Dr. Susan Montoya had just given some shots to a very large but very sleepy Bengal tiger. The doctor saw her family watching through the door window. When she was done, she went out to greet them.

"Okay dad, what's the news?" asked Jonathan.

"I just got a call from the mayor of a town in New York state. Seems they have a bear problem." Mr. Montoya told them what he knew. "Kids, how would you like to spend your spring vacation tracking bears?"

"Huh? You mean it?" They looked at each other with open mouths. "Yes!"

They didn't always get to go on Wildlife Rescue missions. So they jumped at the chance.

"Have you called Jason yet?" Dr. Montoya asked.

"No, I'm going over there now." He looked at his children. "Okay kids, let's go see Uncle Jason. We have a lot of work to do."

Jason Tenbrook wasn't really their uncle, though he was Angela's godfather. Jason was a wildlife biologist. He worked for the United

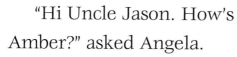

States Forest Service. But today he was at Wildlife Rescue headquarters— a large wooden building on the Montoya's property. They found Jason around back. He was kneeling beside a young deer in a pen.

"Hi Uncle Jason. How's Amber?" asked Angela.

"She's strong as can be. I'm taking her to her new home tomorrow."

Besides being a wildlife biologist, Jason was also a **wildlife rehabilitator.** That meant he took care of wild animals that were sick, injured, or left without a parent to take care of them. When the animals were healthy and strong, Jason took them back to the wilderness. That's where Amber was going.

wildlife rehabilitator – someone who helps injured animals return to the wild

Angela was sad to see her go. "Will she be okay in the woods by herself?"

"Cheer up, Angie," Jason said. "Amber is going where she belongs. Where she'll be happy. Does she look happy in this pen?" Angela had to admit she didn't. "I'm taking her to a friend's place. He has lots of wooded land and doesn't allow hunting. She'll be fine."

He turned to Victor and Susan. "How come you're back from the zoo so early?"

Victor told Jason about the bears. Jason agreed that it was an important mission. The plan was for the Montoyas to drive to New York. They would leave tomorrow, Sunday. Jason would fly the Wildlife Rescue plane later and meet them there on Monday.

Victor and Jason spent the next couple hours checking equipment. Dr. Montoya gathered medical supplies. Angela and Jonathon helped too. They restocked first aid kits and got extra batteries for the flashlights. Mostly they talked about what might happen on the exciting adventure to come.

CHAPTER 3

A Close Call

"One, two, three, up!" Victor grunted as they lifted the last bear trap into the back of the pickup truck. Dr. Montoya wiped the sweat from her forehead. "Wow, those things are heavy. They stack well though."

The weather was dreary, but everyone was cheery this Sunday morning, especially Angela and Jonathan. They walked up to the truck carrying two long, metal poles.

"Where do you want these, dad?" asked Angela.

"Just slide them in next to the traps."

Dr. Montoya checked the medical supplies in her backpack. Victor set the laptop in the front seat. Angela and Jonathan each had their own backpacks. They were filled with books, games, and snacks for the long road trip.

"Okay kids, hop in," said their dad. "Wildlife Rescue is ready to roll."

They were barely on the road 15 minutes. A steady drizzle fell. The road was slick. Angela had just opened a book about bears while Jonathan reached for his handheld video game.

"Deer!" Dr. Montoya cried out.

Dad stepped hard on the breaks. Jonathan's shoulder hit hard against the door as the truck swerved to the left. He looked out in time to see a deer run into the woods. The truck skidded a little on the wet pavement. But Victor kept control of the vehicle. He stopped along the side of the road. Then he let out a deep, slow breath and drove on.

Dr. Montoya turned around. "You kids alright?"

They both nodded, though Jonathan was rubbing his shoulder.

"Let's see, honey." His mom reached back to check his arm. "You'll be okay," she said with a smile. She turned to Victor. "Boy, that deer came out of nowhere."

"Yeah, I was lucky to miss him," said Victor. "Another two inches and we would have all been in trouble."

"I thought deer came out mostly in the evening," said Angela.

"They do," replied her dad. "But you often see them during the day. Especially since all these new roads have been built."

"Huh?" Angela looked confused.

"The roads cut through the deer habitat—all these fields and forests. So the deer have to cross roads in order to get from place to place."

Angela looked at the cover of one of her bear books. "Do you think the same thing is happening with the bears in Mayor Garland's town? You know, new roads and houses being built where the bears live?"

"I wouldn't be surprised," said Victor.

They rode as far as Pittsburgh, Pennsylvania, the first day. By noon the next day, they were winding their way through the wooded Catskill Mountains of New York State. Angela thought it was one of the most beautiful places she had ever seen. The hillsides were covered with forests. The streams sparkled in the sunlight.

But the only black bears she saw were in the pages of her books. She learned a lot about them. Like how they're not always black. Many black bears in the western United States are tan or brown.

Angela had an idea. She decided it would be fun to test her parents. "Okay animal experts. Time for a bear quiz. Question number one. How big are black bears?"

"Well, most males are 150 to 300 pounds," replied their dad. "But some big ones can be 600 pounds or more."

"And most females are 90 to 150 pounds," added their mom.

"Mmm. Okay. . . question two. How long do black bears live?"

Their mom replied quickly. "Usually 10 to 12 years in the wild."

Jonathan wanted to play too. He skimmed a book, then asked, "What do bears eat?"

"Most things," said their dad. "Fruits, seeds, bugs, small mammals, and food in garbage."

"Okay, I got one," said Angela. "How many states have bears living in the wild?"

They both thought a moment. "Umm . . . 25?" guessed their dad.

"Wrong! They live in 40 states." She loved knowing something her parents didn't.

CHAPTER 4

A Bear Plan

After a long drive they finally reached the town. The sign said the population was 500. But that seemed to be changing. They passed a new neighborhood on the edge of town. And a new road led up a hillside where houses were being built.

Mr. Montoya drove straight to the town hall. Jason was already there. They met with the mayor and police chief for about an hour. The Wildlife Rescue team presented several different ways to solve the bear problem.

"Well, you've given us several **options** to consider," said Mayor Garland. "We will discuss them at a town meeting tonight. Then we can vote on it."

----

options – choices

So for the second time in a week, the mayor called an emergency meeting. She contacted the council members, who called the townspeople. Again, the room was packed.

Lauren and Claire Martin were there. When they saw Victor Montoya, they ran up to say hi. Victor was happy to see them. "I understand we wouldn't be here if it wasn't for you," he said as they shook hands.

The girls blushed. Then Lauren whispered, "Mr. Montoya, some people want to kill the bears. They don't have to do that, do they?"

"There are lots of options, Lauren. We'll talk about them all."

During the meeting, Victor explained why they were seeing more bears. "We spent the afternoon exploring the area. We talked with several residents and some of the **state wildlife agencies.** Part of the reason for all the bear visits is that the weather has been drier than usual. The berries aren't growing well, so bears are looking for other sources of food.

"But the main cause of the bear problem is all the new development. Neighborhoods are expanding deeper into bear territory. A few bears have discovered that backyards, garbage cans, and restaurant dumpsters are easy sources of food."

A resident spoke up. "What are we supposed to do? Stop building places to live?"

state wildlife agency – a government office that deals with wildlife issues

Victor could sense tension. "No. I'm just saying that if you spread out into bear territory, you're bound to run into bears more and more. Now, there are several ways to deal with the problem. Jason will explain."

Jason turned the page of a flipchart. He had listed several options. "One thing you can do is take away their food supply in town."

"How do we do that?" asked a resident.

"Several ways. You could soak rags in ammonia and place them in the garbage cans. Bears hate that smell. You could bring in your bird feeders at night. Don't put pet food outside. All these things help, but they won't keep the bears away completely."

Jason went through the other options. The bears could be hunted. Or they could be captured and killed humanely. But Jason made it clear that Wildlife Rescue would not take part in those activities.

"We think the best options are numbers four and five," Jason said pointing to the flipchart. "Based on the tracks I've found and the descriptions from residents, I think there are only three bears. We should be able to capture them. Then we can either release them farther away in the woods or take them out of state."

"Which way is better?" asked one of the council members.

"Well, even if we brought them deep into the Catskills, they still might find their way back.

So I recommend taking them to another state. We could take them to a place in Florida. That state is trying to build up their black bear **population**."

Lauren raised her hand. "Will the bears be able to survive in Florida's climate?" she asked.

"That's an excellent question," replied Jason. "The answer is yes. Black bears **adapt** easily to different climates."

The mayor and the town council voted to relocate the bears to Florida. Angela and Jonathan were happy. So were Lauren and Claire and most of the residents. But a few were not. Angela wasn't sure why. Maybe they wanted to hunt the bears. Or maybe they felt that outsiders were telling them what to do. It's like her mom always said: "When it comes to wildlife problems, you can't please everyone." But it looked like the bears were safe. Now, all they had to do was catch them.

---

population – all the living things of one kind living in an area
adapt – the way an animal acts to help it survive

CHAPTER 5

Look Out!

Wildlife Rescue caught one of the bears sooner than they expected. That night, after the town meeting, someone saw a bear rummaging through a dumpster. The eyewitness called Wildlife Rescue. Victor shot the 200-pound male bear with a drug to make him sleep.

Dr. Montoya put a radio-transmitter collar around his neck. The transmitter gave off a signal so that the bear could be found if it escaped.

The next day, Tuesday, Dr. Montoya kept a close eye on the captured bear. The rest of the Wildlife Rescue team looked for the other bears. Victor and Jonathan were trying to spot bears from the airplane. Jason and Angela were tracking bears in the woods.

"There's another one." Jason pointed out the paw print in the ground. Angela could barely see it. The soil was hard and dry, so a print didn't show up well. But it was clear enough for Jason to see.

Uncle Jason was amazing, Angela thought. No one could track animals like he could. She knew he learned from his grandfather, a Native American. Angela knew that Jason's Native American culture was important to him. Knowing about animals was part of that culture.

Jason stopped by a log that lay across their path. Part of it had been ripped to shreds. Angela bent down. "Wow, looks like a big firecracker went off in this log."

"Not a firecracker, Angie. Those are claw marks. Bears tear into logs to get at the bugs inside. And these claw marks look fresh."

He bent down to look at the log. "These were made some time today. I wonder if . . ."

Jason felt a tap on his shoulder. He looked up and saw Angela looking straight ahead. Looking back, about 50 feet away, was a black bear. A big one.

"What should we do, Uncle Jason?"

"Stay calm. Don't look the bear in the eyes. That might make him nervous."

The bear grunted and slapped the ground with one of it's huge paws. Jason looked back and saw that the truck was not far away.

"Go straight back to the truck, Angie. I'll be there in a minute."

Angela went to the truck and got inside. Just then the bear stood up on two legs. He looked

around. Then he dropped back to all fours. Suddenly the great bear charged toward Jason.

"Uncle Jason!" yelled Angela.

The bear was only 15 feet away when . . . *Whoosh!* He let out a rush of air from his mouth and slammed his front paws into the ground. He came to a sudden stop. Then he turned away and walked off into the woods.

Angela jumped out and ran toward Jason. "Uncle Jason, are you alright? What happened?"

"Bluff charge," replied Jason. "He wasn't really attacking. He was just letting me know that I was too close."

"Should we chase him?" Angela asked.

"No. He's nervous now, and bears can be dangerous if you keep bothering them. Let's go back to the truck and get a trap. We'll set it along this path."

The trap was a long container with bait inside. When the bear tugged at the bait, the trap's door closed.

Jason and Angela dragged the trap into the woods along the bear trail. "This is a good place," announced Jason. "The bear is likely to come through here on its way to town."

Just as they finished setting the bait, the radio on Jason's belt crackled. Victor was checking in. From the airplane Jonathan had spotted a bear in a clearing in the woods. Victor told Jason the location of the bear.

"We're on our way," Victor said into the radio as he walked to the truck.

It was early afternoon by the time Jason and Angela set up the second trap. They put it right in the middle of the clearing where the bear was seen. Then they went back to town.

Everyone met for lunch at a restaurant. Lauren and Claire were there too. Dr. Montoya had invited them to see the bear they caught. The Wildlife Rescue team updated one another on their day so far. Jonathan was excited to hear about the bear's bluff charge.

"Do you think you were near the den?" Lauren asked. "Is that why it charged you?"

"No, the male bear doesn't live in the den," Jason explained. "Only the female does, along with the cubs. The male has to find his own place to live farther away. In the bear world, mamma bear rules." He winked his eye.

"I like the way those bears think," said Angela. Everyone laughed.

The team decided to check the traps at sunset. They reached the first one at 5:30. It was empty. They headed for the second trap, the one in the clearing. The setting sun made the sky glow with orange and pink light. But the woods were starting to get dark.

They were driving around a bend when Jonathan blurted out, "Hey, what's that?"

"I see it too," said Dr. Montoya. "It's a bear. Pull over."

Victor stopped on the side of the road. They could dimly see the bear on the other side of the road. It was coming out of the woods. Victor jumped out and got the rifle out of the back of the truck. It was already loaded—not with bullets but with a **tranquilizing drug** to

tranquilizing drug – a drug that will make a person or animal sleep

make the bear sleep. Victor walked away from the truck to get a clear shot. He stopped and took careful aim. Suddenly a light distracted him from behind. Two headlights were coming around the bend. It was another truck, and it was going fast. The tires kicked up dust and gravel as it passed the Wildlife Rescue truck.

The driver looked at Victor Montoya as he passed him. But he didn't notice the bear that was starting to cross the road up ahead. Angela watched in horror. She could see the bear in the truck's headlights. She stuck her head out the window and yelled at the top of her voice. "LOOK OUT!"

CHAPTER 6

A New Family

The bear stopped when it heard the shout. It started turning back just as the truck swerved to the left. But it was too late. Angela heard the sickening thud as the truck hit the bear's back legs. The bear tumbled to the side of the road.

"Oh no," Angela cried.

Everyone ran to the accident. The bear was alive but in pain. She was trying to get up but couldn't move her back legs. Victor motioned the children to stay back as Dr. Montoya came running with her backpack. She had to give the bear a tranquilizing shot. But the bear was moving too wildly to get close.

"Jason, I need the pole," she said.

He came back quickly with one of the long poles they had packed. Dr. Montoya attached a syringe to the end of it and jabbed it into the bear. Soon, the large animal stopped moving and looked very sleepy. Dr. Montoya moved up to the bear now and gave her a shot of medicine to stop the pain.

The driver had turned the truck around so the headlights lit the scene. He bent over the bear. "Will she be all right?" He said.

"I think so," replied Dr. Montoya. Jason agreed. "It's a good thing you yelled out, Angie," he said.

"Yes, you probably saved the bear's life," said her mom.

"And mine," said the driver. "My truck probably would have tumbled right along with the bear."

He reached out his hand. Angela recognized him from the meeting. He was one of the people who wanted to hunt the bears. Angela smiled and shook his hand. But she wasn't feeling like a hero at the moment. She was too worried about the bear.

It turned out that Angela had nothing to worry about. The bear had a broken leg, but her

mom and Uncle Jason took good care of their
furry patient. The bear would need several
weeks of rehabilitation, where she could get
healthy again.

They caught the last bear in the trap the next
day. Wildlife Rescue now had all three bears.
Jason found the den of the injured bear. It
wasn't far from the clearing where they had set
the trap. He checked the den to see if she had
cubs. She didn't.

The Wildlife Rescue team left town on
Thursday. The mayor and many residents

showed up to thank them. Lauren and Angela exchanged email addresses and promised to keep in touch. "Let us know how Molly does," said Lauren. That's the name she gave the injured bear.

Jason and the Forest Service arranged to fly the bears down to Florida on a cargo plane. Dr. Montoya traveled with them. Victor drove back home. Angela and Jonathon flew to Florida with Jason in the small plane.

The two males were released in the forests of northern Florida. Molly would have to stay in the rehabilitation center until she was well.

Dr. Montoya greeted her children when they arrived at the center. "I have a big surprise for you, kids." She led them to an outside pen. Two bear cubs were playing on a tree trunk. Dr. Montoya handed a cub to each of her children. They cuddled them like teddy bears. But they knew these were real, live, special animals.

"These cubs are orphans. Their mother was killed by a car," she explained. They'll stay here until they can fend for themselves."

Then Jonathan looked at his mom. "Why don't we see if Molly will adopt them?"

"Great idea," said Dr. Montoya. "Female black bears usually are good foster moms."

Later that day, Dr. Montoya and an assistant carefully placed the cubs near a resting Molly. Everyone was nervous, and excited. Would Molly accept the cubs as her own? The little bears playfully tugged at Molly's fur. Then Molly bent down and gently licked the heads of her new cubs.

Black Bears

Black bears live in forests from Florida to Alaska, and Canada to Mexico. In New York state where this story takes place, there are about 6,000 black bears. Wildlife experts think that there are 600,000 black bears in all of North America. Black bears are large and stocky. They have a short tail and small rounded ears. Black bears are not always black. They can be brown and sometimes even white.

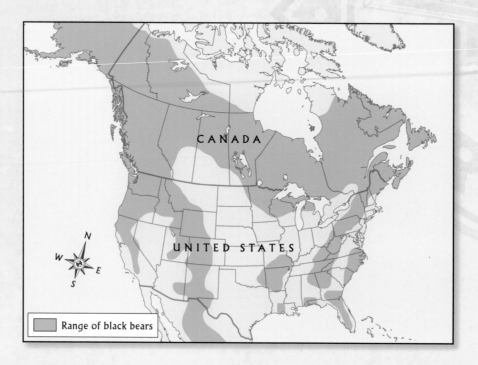

Range of black bears

What Black Bears Eat

Black bears are not picky eaters. They eat what they can find in the forest. In spring, bears use their sharp, curved claws to help them climb trees. They pull down branches and munch on buds and blossoms. Bears also use their claws to tear apart rotten logs. Inside are juicy grubs and other insects. In summer, bears eat tender grasses and berries. They also catch fish. In fall, bears feast on mushrooms, acorns, and other nuts. Bears build up a store of fat over the summer and fall. The extra fat keeps them alive during their winter sleep.

Hibernation

In cold places, black bears sleep most of the winter. This long sleep is called hibernation. To get ready for winter, a black bear finds a hollow log or a cave. It sweeps dried leaves and grass inside to make a bed. Then the bear curls up in its den to sleep. The bear's heartbeat gets slower. The temperature of its body goes down. The bear can hibernate for weeks living off its body fat.

Mother and Cubs

Bear cubs are born in January or February. A mother bear usually has two cubs. The mother bear nurses them and keeps them warm while they grow. When she leads them out of the den in spring, they are able to climb trees. She shows them how to find food. She also protects them from danger. Cubs stay with their mothers for a year and a half.

Write A Class Report

Think about what you have learned about black bears. Write a one-page report about these forest animals.

- Draw a chart like the one below.

- Next to each of the topics, write bear facts you read about.

- Use the chart to write a short class report that will share interesting information about black bears.

Black Bears

What they look like	
Where they live	
What they eat	
How they act	

Read More About Black Bears

Find and read more books about black bears. As you read, think about these questions. They will help you understand more about this topic.

- Are there other types of bears? How are they different from black bears?

- What kinds of wildlife share the forest habitat with black bears?

- What other animals hibernate in winter?

SUGGESTED READING
Reading Expeditions
Life Science: Ecosystems